CONTENTS

H.H. Swami Chinmayananda
With Bal Vihar Children

Tell Me A Story - 3

Adapted by
Swamini Sharda Priyananda
and
Bharati Sukhtankar

Design and Visuals
Nina Bahl

CENTRAL CHINMAYA MISSION TRUST
MUMBAI - 400 072

© Central Chinmaya Mission Trust, Mumbai

Total no. Of copies printed till   - 2008   -   29,000 copies
Revised Edition October   - 2009   -   3,000 copies

Published by:
CENTRAL CHINMAYA MISSION TRUST
Sandeepany Sadhanalaya,
Saki Vihar Road,
Mumbai - 400 072, INDIA.
Tel.: 91-22-2857 2367 / 2828 / 5806 / 6919
Fax: 91-22-2857 3065
E-mail: ccmt@vsnl.com
Website: www.chinmayamission.com

Distribution Centre in USA:
CHINMAYA MISSION WEST
Publication Division
560 Bridgetown Pike,
Langhorne, PA 19053, USA.
Tel: (215) 396-0390
Fax: (215) 396-9710
E-mail: Publications@chinmaya.org
Website:www.chinmayapublications.org

Design and Visuals
Nina Bahl

Printed by :
JAK Printers Pvt Ltd.

Price : Rs. 125.00

ISBN : 9788175974289

Gurudev on Storytelling...

Story telling is an art that should be cultivated by all parents. There is a treasure of joy for the storyteller and a heritage of good that the innocent tiny listener can gain from the story that is told to them. Children can be readily held in attention only by the mesmeric enchantment of the rhythm in the movements of the theme of the story.

While listening to the story a child is in a different mode as children alone can be. They are thrilled by their love for the fantasia. Their imagination lights up and their wide eyed joys are kindled. Children are at such moments in the very lap of Nature gliding on incredible patterns surging in their own hearts.

The very story in the growing child will by itself instill the great truths and higher values of life as time passes on. Tell, never teach a story. Children learn more by a story well told than what we teach them through a story.

Publisher's Note

CCMT Publications Division has great pleasure in releasing **Tell me a Story III** in its redesigned format adding beautiful visuals to the folk tales. They are specially designed to capture the imagination of our children. The hidden values come alive and talk to us through the imagery. We are thankful to Swamini Shardapriyananda and Bharati Sukhtankar for having initially compiled the stories. We are sure that this book will help children and their parents in imbibing the finer values of life that the stories project.

Mahashivratri   **Central Chinmaya Mission Trust**
March 6, 2008
Mumbai

POSTPONEMENT

The Pandavas ruled justly and generously over Indraprastha. Yudhishthira (Dharamaraja) was the king. It was usual for many people to attend Dharmaraja's court during the day, to meet him. They sought his guidance in solving their problems and asked him for whatever help they needed.

One day Bhima saw a Brahmin going to visit Dharmaraja and returning after a short while. He looked sad and was empty-handed, so Bhima concluded that he had not received anything from his elder brother.

Concerned, Bhima asked him, "Sir, you are returning empty-handed. Have you met my brother? Shall I take you to him?" The Brahmin was pleased at this courteous enquiry from Bhima. He replied, "Yes, indeed, I have met your brother, the King. I asked him for something but he has asked me to come tomorrow. He promised to give it to me tomorrow."

Bhima was surprised. His elder brother, postponing a good deed till the next day! He thought for a minute and smiled. Then he went to the big drum kept at the main gate and started

beating the drum thunderously. The drum at the main gate was not usually used. It was meant for special, occasions when something very important had to be announced. It was a summons for everyone in the palace to stop doing whatever work they might be engaged in and rush to the main gate.

As the drumbeats sounded, like roll upon roll of thunder, under the powerful hand of Bhimasena, everyone quickly gathered around him, in response to his urgent summons. Dharmaraja hurried towards the main gate

from his court, Draupadi from the inner chambers, Arjuna from his weapons, the twins from the stables. All people big and small gathered there. Still Bhima did not stop beating the drum. He struck the drum with great vigour, till Dharmaraja put a hand on his shoulder and said, "You can stop now, Bhima. All of us are here. Now please tell us why you have summoned us so urgently."

Bhima saluted his elder brother and then turned towards the others who had gathered there. "I have called you all here to make an important announcement about the greatest victory of our elder brother Dharamraja. This victory is so great that all of us should rejoice and celebrate it."

Dharmaraja was surprised. What victory was Bhima talking of? He had not even left the palace to go out that day. He could not imagine how he could have had any victory. Turning to Bhima, he asked in bewilderment, "What are you talking about, Bhima? I have had no victory at all today. Are you dreaming?"

Bhima laughed uproariously and said,

"Really, you don't even know your greatness, brother. Let me announce your victory. Listen all of you, my brothers and kinsfolk. Today our brother has conquered the unconquerable death. Who else can have a greater victory than this?

When this Brahmin asked for a favour, Dharmaraja promised to give it to him tomorrow. He has asked him to come again tomorrow. Is this not a wonderful victory? Our brother is sure that he will be alive till tomorrow and that the Brahmin will also be alive until tomorrow. If only all of us could be as sure of our life as he is!"

Hearing Bhima's words, Dharmaraja realised his mistake. He said, "Yes, Bhima, you are right to remind me of my duty. Postponement of a good deed is deplorable. I should not have done it."

He then invited the Brahmin into the palace and gave him what he needed. The Brahmin left with a smile of contentment, showering blessings on the wise and generous king.

HEAVEN AND HELL

Heaven and hell are both created here on earth by our actions. There is no hell except our selfishness. There is no heaven other than our own selfless love for others.

Once a group of people wanted to know what makes the difference between hell and heaven. The place where all suffer, is called hell and where all enjoy bliss is called heaven. So the committee of people wanting to know how hell is made, first went to hell where all the residents suffered untold agonies. What they saw in hell surprised them very much. Hell looked like a very rich place where every enjoyable luxury was available in plenty. Why should any one suffer here, they wondered?

As it was lunch time, all the denizens of hell were gathered in the dining hall. The committee went there to investigate whether there was any problem with the food. Again, what met their eyes surprised them beyond words. The dining table was loaded with an abundance of various delicacies. Obviously no one need starve for lack of food! Yet the most puzzling thing of all was the fact that all the hell dwellers, who were gathered there, looked famished, hungry and angry. They were quarrelling and shouting abusively at each other.

The investigation committee curiously scrutinised the jostling, quarrelling, fighting throng of people. They were amazed to see that none of them had any elbow joints in their arms. Therefore they were unable to bend their hands and feed themselves, even though plenty of food was available. So all of them starved amidst plenty and were utterly miserable.

The committee felt that this was a cruel joke to play upon the people of hell. Why give them plenty of food if they couldn't eat it?

They wished to see how things were in heaven and reached there in time to see the heavenly beings at lunch. Heaven was exactly like hell. It looked very rich. It was full of every imaginable luxury and all the enjoyable things of life. As they approached the dining hall, they could hear happy cheers of satisfaction and joy emanating from there. The committee members hastened to the hall to witness such exuberant joy! The dining table was loaded with delicacies, just as in hell. The people looked happy, well fed and content. They were eating happily. Now the committee members looked carefully at their arms. Here too, the arms of the residents were without elbow joints. They too could not bend their forearms to feed themselves. Still they were in a blissfully happy state, with not even a trace of unhappiness on their serene faces.

In heaven everyone understood that the plentiful and delicious food in front of them, was not given to them to eat selfishly by themselves, but was to be served lovingly to those around them. So they all filled their plates with delicacies from the table and happily fed each other. Since each one lovingly fed the other, all of them got plenty to eat, and nobody starved. Everyone was blissfully happy and it became heaven. In hell the unfortunate beings could not understand that their hands were meant to serve their fellow-beings. When they repeatedly tried to feed only themselves, they couldn't, and it became a living hell.

GOD'S GIFT

Once upon a time in a small village there lived a farmer. He was a great devotee of God, content with what he had and never craving for the material pleasures of life. His wife was not as much of a devotee but she also lived simply without whining for the luxuries of life. They had a small field in which the farmer cultivated a few crops for their simple needs.

One day, when the farmer was tilling the land, he uncovered an earthen jar which had been buried under the ground. Lifting it out carefully the farmer opened the lid and looked in. The jar was filled with shiny gold coins! Replacing the lid, the farmer put the jar under a nearby tree and continued his work. He worked till evening and returned home as usual, without even glancing at the jar. At night, while eating dinner, he remembered the jar and mentioned it to his wife. His wife was shocked. "What a simpleton you are!" she cried. "You did not seek the wealth but it came to you as God's gift. Why didn't you bring it home?"

The farmer smiled and said, "If it is God's gift to me, it will remain there tomorrow also. Why worry?"

As the couple was talking, two thieves, who were waiting to loot the house after the couple went to sleep, overheard the conversation. "What a fool this farmer is!" they exclaimed in amazement. "Anyway it's good that we heard about the treasure. We won't need to break into the farmer's house now. Let us go to the field and pick up the jar." So deciding, they silently crept away from there. Reaching the field, they searched for the tree under which the farmer had found the jar. There, to be sure, was the jar. They picked it up in great glee. It was very heavy, but they didn't mind the weight, because they would have plenty of gold to share. Silently they melted into the night, before anyone could see and stop them. They took to their heels and ran as fast as they could with the jar, until they reached a deserted place where there was no danger of their being seen. Tingling with excitement they placed the jar on the ground, and opened the lid. But what they saw in the jar turned their blood into water! Instead of the gold they had expected to find, they saw live cobras hissing and writhing inside the jar. Panic stricken, the thieves replaced the lid quickly and ran away from there as fast as their legs would carry them.

The next night, they returned to the farmer's house to discover what the truth was. The farmer had said there was gold in the jar. Then how had the cobras got in? What had happened to the gold? They were anxious to get to the bottom of the matter.

The farmer was eating his dinner. He told his wife that the jar was not under the tree where he had left it the previous day. His wife was sad at the loss. "You ought to have brought it yesterday itself. We have lost the gold, because you are such a simpleton," she wailed. The farmer smiled and said, "Well, the fact that the jar was not there proves that it was not God's gift to us. Then why worry about what is not ours?"

When the thieves heard this conversation, they were unable to decide whether the farmer was really a simpleton, who believed what he said, or whether he had cleverly outsmarted them and wanted to get rid of them by making them take away the jar of cobras. They felt they should check this out, and wreak their vengeance on the farmer if he had tricked them. So they returned to the spot where they had abandoned the jar the previous night, heard the cobras hissing inside and carefully carried it back to the tree in the farmer's field. If the farmer was innocent, he would open the jar. If he wasn't, he would not open the jar.

The next night they returned again to the farmer's house to hear what had happened that day. The farmer was eating his dinner. He said to his wife, "Eh, today the jar came back to the tree." The wife beamed with pleasure. "Oh, good. You are now sure that it is God's gift to us. Did you bring it home?" she asked.

"Oh, no," said the farmer. "If it is God's gift to us, why should I carry it home? It will come by itself."

The thieves were listening carefully to this conversation. When the farmer said that he had not touched the jar, their suspicions that the farmer had deliberately misled them were confirmed. They grew very angry and wanted to punish the farmer. In the dark of night, they went to the field, and found the jar under the tree. Hearing the hissing of the cobras inside, they carefully carried the jar up to the door of the farmer's house and put it there. They wanted to see what the farmer would do in the morning. Even if the farmer did not open it, his wife was sure to do so and get bitten by the cobras. They spent the whole night in eager anticipation of the events of the next morning.

Early next morning at daybreak, the farmer opened his door to go to his field. The moment the door opened, his eyes fell on the jar. He smiled and called his wife, "My dear, come and see. Here is God's gift at our doorstep."

The wife came running and lifted the lid. Her eyes danced with joy to see all the gold inside. Looking admiringly at her husband, she said, "You were right. What God meant for us, nobody can take away. It has ultimately reached us." She picked up the jar and took it inside.

The unfortunate thieves were stunned at this turn of events and at a loss to understand what had happened! What became of the cobras in the jar? Why could they not see the gold, if it was really there in the jar? They did not know that to steal what God had meant for others was as dangerous as stealing a jar of poisonous cobras.

THE WAY TO LEARN

When the Pandavas and the Kauravas were young boys, they were all sent to an ashram to study. Besides them there were several other princes too, who had also been sent to be educated there. There was keen competition among them all, to be the best in studies and win the teacher's praise. They were making good progress in their studies and the teacher was happy with his pupils.

One day the teacher had to go out on some work. He expected to be away for several days. So he called all his students and gave them a few lessons to be studied during his absence. The teacher left and the students were left to their individual pursuits for the time being.

A fortnight later the teacher returned. When the class met, the teacher asked how they had spent their time during his absence and what they had studied. Each prince came forward and explained how diligently and sincerely he had studied. One had learnt three lessons, another four, and yet another five. The teacher beamed at them as one by one the pupils stood up and gave an account of themselves. At last it was Dharmaraja's turn. The teacher looked at him expectantly as he was the most industrious of all his pupils. Dharmaraja said in a low voice, "I have studied only one sentence, Sir." The teacher was stunned. He could hardly believe his ears. "Just one sentence?" he asked. "Yes Sir,

I could study only one sentence in such a short time," Dharmaraja repeated.

What had come over Dharmaraja? The teacher could not understand why he required a full fortnight to learn one sentence. Dharmaraja was older than all his other pupils. He ought to have been more diligent in his studies and set an example to the others. But here was the boy shamelessly declaring that a fortnight was not sufficient to study more than a single sentence.

If he tolerated such insolence from the oldest boy, the others might follow his example and be lazy in future. The teacher looked around the class to see how the other students were taking it. They were looking on with derisive smiles on their lips, eager to see how the teacher would react, because they knew that Dharmaraja was his favourite pupil. Would the teacher punish Dharmaraja or would he overlook his favourite disciple's laziness? The teacher understood what they were thinking. He did not want to give the impression that he was partial to any boy. He looked sternly at Dharmaraja and said, "Aren't you ashamed of yourself? The others who are so much younger than you, have studied much more than you have."

Dharmaraja's face remained serene and tranquil. "No, Sir, I couldn't help it. This is all I could finish."

The teacher lost his temper. "What a big fool you are!" he shouted. "You are not only lazy but brazen too. Are you not ashamed?" Still Dharmaraja remained calm and tranquil. "I am sorry to disappoint you, Sir. This is all I could study." All the pupils burst into laughter. The teacher could not control himself. He felt that he must put a stop to Dharmaraja's stubbornness and set an example for the others. In a rush of anger he gave Dharmaraja a hard slap with his outstretched hand. Dharmaraja's delicate cheek grew crimson under the hard blow. Still he remained calm and cool, and said in a low voice, "I am sorry to disappoint you, Sir, I could study only this much."

Again the shameless assertion! The teacher raised his hand once more and gave him another blow. Dharmaraja still retained his composure. The teacher gave him yet another slap. But Dharmaraja remained calm and quiet, not trying to shield himself, not protesting or even justifying himself. The class looked on in amazement and the teacher also stopped, wondering at Dharmaraja's calmness. It dawned on him that Dharmaraja had achieved something extraordinary here. He looked searchingly into the calm, unperturbed eyes of the boy and asked, "My son, what was the sentence that you have learnt?"

Dharmaraja brought out his book and showed him the sentence. The teacher read it, "Don't ever be angry!" The teacher repeated the sentence aloud, "Don't ever be angry!" In a flash the teacher and all the pupils understood what Dharmaraja had achieved. His study was not the lip study of the others but it was a practical application of what he had read.

The teacher's eyes filled with tears when he realised how sincerely Dharmaraja had applied himself to his lesson. He embraced the boy and said in a choked voice, "My son, please pardon me for having done you an injustice. Today you have taught me how lessons should be studied. If everyone was like you, the world would have been a heaven on earth."

ARJUNA'S CONCENTRATION

Long, long ago, when the Pandavas and the Kauravas were boys, they learnt archery from Guru Dronacharya. One day the *Acharya* arranged a shooting demonstration as a test of his disciples' skills. The parents, visitors and archery enthusiasts all gathered to see how the princes were progressing. Dronacharya placed a wooden bird in the branches of a tree which was half a mile away. The visitors were seated on either side and the pupils stood in a line facing the tree on which the bird was placed. A line was drawn in front of the pupils, and a bow and arrow were kept beside it. The pupils' eager faces were turned to the teacher. They were impatient to know what the test was going to be and were itching to show off their skills.

Stepping forward to explain the test, Dronacharya said, "Listen, princes. On the left branch of that tree, you can see a wooden bird. You have to stand on this line in front of you and shoot the eye of the bird with this bow and arrow. Are you ready?" All of them nodded their heads. "Good," the teacher said, "first, let Dharmaraja come forward and shoot."

Dharmaraja stood on the line, took up the bow and arrow and aimed. "Sir, may I shoot?" he asked the *Acharya*. The *Acharya* scrutinised the position in which Dharmaraja was standing holding the bow. "Dharmaraja, can you see me?" Dharmaraja nodded his head and said, "Yes, teacher, I see you clearly." Dronacharya smiled and said softly, "Dharmaraja, put down the bow and go back. You can't hit the bird." Dharmaraja flushed with shame. He put down the bow and went back to his place.

Then it was Bhimasena's turn. He came forward, lifted up the bow and took aim. Dronacharya asked, "Bhima, can you see the visitors on either side?" Bhima said, "Yes, Sir, I can see them all though not very clearly." Dronacharya shook his head. "Bhima, go back.

You can't shoot the bird." Bhimasena was puzzled. Yet an order was an order. So he put down the bow and walked back.

Next, Duryodhana came forward and took up the bow. He aimed at the bird and then turning towards the *Acharya*, asked, *"Acharya, may I shoot?"* The *Acharya* shook his head and said, "Don't, it will be a waste of time. Go back to your place." Duryodhana's face flamed red with indignation. He flung the bow down angrily and walked back.

One by one all the princes came forward and prepared to shoot. The *Acharya* would ask them a question, listen to the answer and send them back. Everyone was surprised and they started murmuring, "The *Acharya* is very strict. He is not satisfied with anyone. Will even a single student be able to please him?"

At last, it was Arjuna's turn to aim. He came forward, stood at the line and fixed the arrow to the bow. Dronacharya keenly observed Arjuna. He asked, "Arjuna, are you ready to shoot?"

"Yes, Sir, I am ready." replied Arjuna. "

"Arjuna, do you see me?"

"No, Sir."

"Do you see your brothers and the visitors?"

"No, Sir."

"Do you see the tree and the branch on which the bird is kept?"

"No, Sir."

Dronacharya smiled happily. "Arjuna, do you see the bird?"

"No, Sir."

The visitors and the princes were all puzzled. If Arjuna did not see the bird, how could he ever hit it? But the *Acharya's* smile broadened even more. He asked eagerly —

"Arjuna, what do you see?"

Arjuna replied, "*Acharya*, I see the eye of the bird which has to be shot."

Dronacharya nodded his head appreciatively and said, "Good, Arjuna, shoot!"

Arjuna pulled the string of the bow taut, until it touched his ear and shot. The arrow flew forward in a straight line without wavering and hit the eye of the bird. There was thunderous applause from the visitors. That day the princes learnt a new lesson on the importance of concentration.

THE GREEDY BARBER

Once upon a time there was a barber who worked for a king. He was a good barber, skilled in shaving and very sincere too. The king, well satisfied by his service retained him for a number of years and grew very fond of him. The barber also loved his king and served him with great care. His cottage was on the other side of a small forest adjoining the palace. The barber had to pass through the forest every day in order to reach the palace and again walk back through it after his duty was over.

One day the barber was walking home thinking of his good fortune in having a kind-hearted king as his employer. Suddenly he heard a voice from nowhere, "O barber, do you want a lot of gold, diamonds and costly jewels?"

The barber started in fright. This wasn't the voice of an ordinary human being, it sounded eerie and hollow. His eyes darted in all directions to see where the voice was coming from, but there was no one to be seen. He thought that it must be some sort of spirit. Frightened, he started running to escape being caught by the spirit. "O barber, I am a *yaksha*. Do you want a lot of wealth, gold, and diamonds?" the voice asked again loudly. The barber ran faster. The voice pursued him with the same query again and again. "O barber, do you want jars and jars of gold, diamonds and

precious stones?" The barber was out of breath now, but still he ran even faster. As the voice kept repeating the question, he felt tempted. He thought,"Even if it is a spirit that offers it, wealth is wealth. Why should I not take it? I am a poor man and wealth will give me a lot of happiness." He kept running and panted,"Yes, I want... I want a lot of wealth... gold and diamonds." By now he had reached the end of the forest. In great relief he slowed down to a walk as he neared his house and opened the door. Lo and behold! There stood seven huge jars which he had never seen before. Had the promised wealth already been sent? With a thumping heart, he went near the jars and

peeped in. His head reeled at the dazzling splendour that met his eyes. The jars were full to the brim with shining gold coins, glittering jewels and diamonds. He picked up a few diamonds and examined them in the sunlight, streaming through the window.

Because of his long years of service in the palace, he knew what real jewels looked like. He could see that all these jewels were real and expensive. What luck! Unasked, all this wealth had come to him gifted by some unknown God. Surely, he was going to be very, very happy with such riches. He had no children. There was just his wife and himself. With this immense wealth he would not even have to work.

As he was thus musing and examining jar after jar, his wife came in from the kitchen. She saw what her husband was doing and asked in surprise, "Where did you get these jars from? How did you get all those diamonds?"

The barber explained how he had heard the voice in the forest, how he had accepted its offer and how he had found the jars on reaching home. "You have been in the house all this while. Did you hear any sound? The jars must have been brought in by somebody." The wife shook her head. She had not heard anything at all. Nevertheless, she was as pleased with the riches as her husband and together they started to examine them. All the jars were full, except the seventh one. The seventh one was only one-fourth full. The couple looked at each other in dismay. "What a pity!" the wife exclaimed, "You must have come in too soon and disturbed our unknown benefactor. You ran unnecessarily. Had you come walking slowly, the invisible god would have had the time to fill this jar too." She sighed unhappily. "That is why they say, slow and steady wins the race. You were too fast."

Her reasoning appeared sound to the barber. "Yes," he admitted ruefully, "I did run fast. It must have been a hard job for him to carry all the jars here and fill them up one by one. Had I walked slowly, the seventh jar would have been full too. How unfortunate we are!" Sighing, he wept and blamed himself again and again. The wife also shed tears and wailed, "How unlucky we are! Our unknown benefactor ought to have warned you not to return too soon. O, why did he not tell you to

wait for some time, and then come home?"
They held on to each other and wept again.

Thus they grieved for this lapse till the
evening. By that time they had both reached a
decision, "Let us gather enough money to
purchase gold and diamonds and fill the empty
jar!" they said.

The barber then went to the king and
begged, "O King, we are poor and can hardly
make both ends meet. May I request you to
increase my salary?"

The king was surprised. He knew that the
barber had no children and that his salary was
more than sufficient for his needs. Still, as it was
the first request made by his favourite barber,
the king agreed to double his salary. The barber
was happy.

But at the end of six months, they still did
not have enough to fill the seventh jar.

The barber again approached the king with
another request to increase his salary. The king
was very puzzled. A second raise within six

months! What was he doing with all this money? Looking at him long and shrewdly, the king asked, "Another raise? In all your service this is the first time you have started asking for more money. Are you filling the seventh jar of the *yaksha* or what?"

The barber was stunned. That was exactly what he was doing. How could the king know about the *yaksha* and the seven jars? Was the *yaksha* playing a trick on him? Troubled by these thoughts, he told the king the whole story.

The king looked at him in pity and said, "I suspected something of the sort. Or else why should you, a happy, healthy man be reduced to a pale, woebegone shadow of yourself? Do you think that the *yaksha* gave you all this wealth for you to enjoy? He gave it mischievously to kill you with anxiety and greed. The six jars of gold are more than enough to last you and your wife till the end of your lives. But you won't be satisfied with what you have. You will worry about what you haven't got in the seventh jar. The *yaksha* knows how greedy the human mind is and he gave you the seven jars only to kill you both. Can't you see how you have been suffering ever since you got these riches?"

The truth of what the king said went home and in a sudden flash the barber understood what had happened. He knew that he had lost his sleep, peace, contentment, health and joy during these last six months. It wouldn't be long before he and his wife died of broken hearts.

He entreated the king to help him escape from the *yaksha's* clutches.

The king said, "If you want to escape from his clutches, the only way is to return the jars. He cannot leave the jars in your house unless you want them. Once he had asked me too, whether I wanted wealth, just as he asked you. Instead of accepting it, I asked him a counter question, as to whether he was offering the wealth for my enjoyment or my suffering. He did not reply. As I did not accept his offer, he could not bring the jars into my palace. Today, when you go home through the forest, shout loudly that you don't need his riches and that he can take back his jars. All of them will disappear by the time you reach home."

The barber followed the king's advice and doing what he had been told, reached home. When he opened the door, he found the seven jars were gone. Now, the barber did not grieve, because a great weight had been lifted from his mind. His peace had returned. The greed took with it his worry, when it went. He and his wife were happy and content once more!

THE ELDER BROTHER

Once upon a time a widow lived with her only son in a small village. They were very poor and could not afford to live in luxury. They had a small hut adjoining a forest. Their village being very small, there was no school for children. On the other side of the forest was a larger village which had a school. So the widow had to send her son to that school. He was the only boy going to that school from his village. Every day he had to walk alone through the forest to reach his school.

The boy used to feel terribly afraid while walking alone in the forest and often said so to his mother. The poor mother, what could she do? She was a great devotee of Lord Krishna.

She fervently prayed to God to help her son. One day the boy was so afraid that he refused to go to school and started crying. His mother embraced him, wiped his tears and said, "My son, don't be afraid of the forest. Would I send you alone there, if there was any danger? In the forest lives your elder brother Gopal, who has promised to look after you. So, whenever you feel frightened, call out to your brother. He will surely come and keep you company in the forest." "Really, mother? Have I got a brother who lives in the forest? What does he do there? Why can't he come home and live with us here?" The boy's excited questions tumbled out. The mother smiled and said, "My dear, your brother looks after the cattle in the forest. That is why he does not get time to come home. But don't worry. He will surely come whenever you call out to him."

Now the boy felt reassured. He wasn't frightened any more. He couldn't wait to meet his elder brother and see what he was like. He ate his food and eagerly went running into the forest to meet his brother. Once he had reached the depths of the forest he cried out, "Gopal, my brother, please come out. I am anxious to see you." He waited for some time. No one came. He called out once again. Still no response. A third time. No one came. He grew very frightened and cried out tearfully, "Brother, where are' you? Mother told me that you would surely come to me. I am very frightened. Please come quickly." He cried out trembling in fright. Lo! From out of the forest dashed a young boy, with a blue complexion, wearing a yellow dhoti, a peacock feather in his hair. He had a bewitching smile on his lips. He looked a little older than the boy and said, "O

brother, I just heard your cry and came running. Why are you crying? Has not Mother told you that I am here?"

The boy was thrilled to know he had such a handsome brother. Holding Gopal's hands he gazed at him in rapture. Gopal smiled and asked, "What are you looking at?" The boy laughed in sheer joy and said, "O my brother, I never knew that I had a brother until Mother told me this morning. How handsome you are! Why do you never come home?" Gopal smiled and said gently, "Did not Mother tell you that I am working here? I am always busy. But I shall

always come whenever you are in the forest and call out to me. Let us go now. It is time for your school." Hand in hand they walked together. Gopal knew the names of all the trees and birds in the forest. He pointed them all out as they walked along. The boy was so engrossed with this wonderful brother of his, that he never noticed where they were walking. When the forest ended, Gopal said, "Look, we have reached the village. There is your school. Now I shall go back." But the boy did not want to lose sight of his brother. He clung to Gopal and begged him to go to school with him. Gopal shook his head, "I have to tend the cows. How can I attend school? Don't worry. I shall meet you in the forest in the evening." The boy let him go with great reluctance. The whole day he thought of this wonderful brother of his. How lucky he was to have such a brother! He waited impatiently for the evening to come, for he was eager to be with his brother again.

As soon as the school closed, he rushed to the forest and called out aloud. "Gopal, Gopal, I have come. Do you hear me!" The blue boy came running and laughing. They embraced each other lovingly and walked towards the boy's village. As they reached the village and the forest ended, Gopal turned to go back. The boy parted from him only after repeated assurances from Gopal that he would surely meet him again the next day. The boy ran home, bursting with the news of his new-found brother. His mother listened to his tale in wonder and gratitude. From the description of Gopal that her son gave, she had no doubt that Lord Krishna Himself had come to protect her son in the forest. She shed grateful tears and prayed to the Lord to look after her son.

Now the boy no longer feared the forest. He would rush out of the house even before it was time for him to go to school, because he was eager to spend as much time as possible with his brother. In his brother's company he did not know how time flew. Gradually the year came to an end and the teacher's birthday approached. It was the custom for each student to bring some present for the teacher on his birthday. The boy was worried. In the evening he asked his mother what he could give to the teacher. Poor mother! She had nothing at home she could offer. At last she said, "Why don't you ask your brother

Gopal when you meet him tomorrow? He will surely suggest something."

The next day as they were walking through the forest, the boy asked Gopal whether he could give him something for his teacher's birthday. Gopal replied, "I am not very rich. But don't worry, I shall try to get something tomorrow." The boy was happy. He slept peacefully that night. The next day he met Gopal eagerly. Sure enough, Gopal hadn't forgotten his promise. He took out a small pot of curd from his bag and gave it to the boy. It

was a very small pot but the boy was happy. He wouldn't have to go empty-handed to school.

Inside the school everything wore a festive look. There were no classes that day. The students along with their parents had gathered and several rich presents were given to the teacher. The teacher smiled. Someone brought a bag of rice, another a cow, a third one some fruit and a fourth loads of flowers. The school was filled with the presents. Looking at all the rich presents brought by the others, the boy felt ashamed. He had brought such a tiny present! What would the teacher think? Would the other pupils laugh at him? Fearful of their mockery, the boy stood in one corner, not daring to approach the teacher and hiding the small pot of curd under his shirt.

One by one the children came forward offering their presents. The teacher received them with a smile and a kind word. He observed the boy shyly standing in a corner, hiding something under his shirt. He knew that the boy's mother was a poor widow who couldn't afford to send any present, nor did he expect anything from her. He taught all his students out of love, irrespective of their wealth. When he saw that the boy had brought something which he was hesitant to show, he called out with an encouraging smile, "Son, why are you standing there? Come forward and show me what you have brought for me."

The boy slowly moved forward and brought out the tiny pot from under his shirt. His face grew crimson with shame at the thought that his friends would make fun of him. As he offered the tiny pot to the teacher, there were some sniggers of suppressed laughter. But the kindly teacher received the pot from him and said, "How thoughtful of you to have brought such shining white curd. Thank you very much." He poured the curd into the big pot of curd brought by some other pupil and was about to throw the empty pot out of the window. Suddenly his hand stopped and he stared at the pot in disbelief. Instead of being empty, the pot was again full of curd. Surprised, he poured the curd into the big pot again and looked at the small pot. Lo! The tiny pot was again full of shining white curd. Again he poured it out. Again the pot was full. The whole class and all the elders who had gathered there looked on in wonderment. The teacher again and again emptied the pot and it got filled again and again. The boy also looked on in fascination. He never knew that his brother Gopal had given him such a fine gift for his teacher. His heart swelled with pride, as the others looked at him with new respect. He knew that thanks to his brother, his was the best gift offered that day.

The teacher was puzzled. He looked at the boy and asked, "My dear boy, where did you get this magic pot from?" The boy answered, "My brother Gopal gave it to me, Sir." "Brother!" exclaimed the teacher, "You have no brothers. Which brother is this?" "I have no brother at home, Sir," replied the boy. "It is my brother Gopal, who lives in the forest. He has given me the pot."

Then the whole story came tumbling out. When the teacher heard the description of Gopal, he knew at once that the boy's brother was none other than the Divine Cowherd Himself. He shed tears of ecstasy and asked the boy in a choked voice, "Son, will you take me to your brother?" The boy was eager to introduce his unique brother to one and all. He readily agreed to take the teacher to his brother in the forest. Not only the teacher but all the others who were there wished to have a vision of the Divine Brother. Everyone followed the boy to the forest. "Gopal, my brother Gopal, please come. My teacher, classmates, and several elders have come to see you. Please come quickly." The boy waited for some time. Gopal did not come. Thinking that his brother must have gone far today, and hadn't heard him, the boy

called out louder and again yet louder. Still there was no response. He was very disappointed. With tears in his eyes, he begged, "Gopal, are you angry with me for bringing these people without your permission? Please do not be angry with me. If you don't appear before them they will not believe me and think of me as a liar. Please come, only this once." There came a voice from afar. "No, brother, I am not angry with you. I love you very much. But your teacher and the others can't see Me. You alone can see Me, not the others."

Everyone heard the Divine voice. The teacher's eyes filled with tears. He embraced the boy and said, "Son, it is true. We are not pure enough to have a vision of the Lord. You are pure in mind and simple in faith. That is why you could get His darshan. We too, are lucky to have heard His voice. Thank you very much, my dear boy. Hereafter, it will be my life's purpose to make myself as pure as you, so that one day I shall be fit to have a darshan of the Lord."

IN DEVOTION IS WISDOM

Once upon a time a monkey lived in the branches of a rose-apple tree. The tree was huge and always had a number of ripe rose apples. The monkey ate the fruit with relish, jumped to and fro on the branches and enjoyed his life. Despite his merry life, the monkey was very devoted and prayed to Lord Rama with great fervour. One could always hear him singing, "*Om Sri Ram Jaya Ram Jaya Jaya Ram!*"

As the monkey jumped up and down on the branches, swinging to and fro, some ripe fruit would fall into the river below the tree. One day, a crocodile swimming in the river swallowed a rose-apple as it fell in the water. It tasted good. The crocodile ate all the fruit that fell from the tree above. When he had finished, he raised his head to see from where it had come. Up in the branches he saw the monkey swinging by his tail and singing. The crocodile said, "O monkey, I like your song and I like the fruit you dropped. Will you be my friend?" The monkey liked the crocodile's sincerity. He agreed cheerfully, "Yes, let's be friends."

Their friendship gradually grew. The crocodile was attracted by the simple, devout life of the monkey. He started spending more and more time in his company and almost forgot his wife at home. Even when he went home he sang the praises of his new friend. As the days went by, the crocodile's wife got fed up of this new fascination of her husband. She thought that if she didn't do something about it fast, her husband would one day abandon her altogether. So she hatched a vicious plot to get rid of the monkey.

One night, when the crocodile returned home after many happy hours of talk with the monkey, his wife tied a cloth round her head and lay moaning and groaning. The crocodile was alarmed. He asked, "My dear, why are you groaning? Are you feeling ill? Shall I get you some medicine?" The wife groaned some more and mumbled, "What is the use of telling you anything? Do you care for me at all? Even if I drop dead it will not make a difference to you."

At this accusation, the poor crocodile protested, "How unjust you are, my dear. Don't I love you more than myself? I am prepared to sacrifice anything, even my life for your sake. Believe me!" The wife moaned as if she were in great pain and said, "If you really love me, now is the time to prove it. Since the morning I am suffering from a severe headache. I consulted a doctor who said that there was only one remedy for this headache. If you have any regard for me you will immediately get that medicine for me."

The husband eagerly asked, "Please tell me quickly what the medicine is. Whatever it is, I will get it for you." The wife smiled inwardly. She groaned once more and said, "O, the medicine is something which you can easily get, if you wish to get it. The doctor said that a monkey's heart has to be made into a paste and applied on my forehead. I will then get rid of this headache once and for all."

The husband recoiled in horror. "A monkey's heart? How can I get it? It's impossible!" The wife moaned shedding bitter tears. She exclaimed, "See, I knew you would say that. Your friend means more to you than even my life. All right, go and spend time with your friend. I shall moan, groan and die here, all alone and uncared for!" She sighed deeply and turned away from her husband sobbing bitterly. This was too much for the crocodile. He came near her, wiped her tears and said, "Please don't say such things. I am prepared to bring you my

friend's heart. But how can I get it? I can hardly ask him to come down the tree so that I can take his heart, can I?"

The wife replied, "No you can hardly do that. But you can do one thing. Go and invite the monkey to our house for lunch tomorrow. Ask him to jump on your back and carry him here. Once he is here I shall kill him and take out his heart." The husband felt very sad when he heard how he had to deceive his best friend. Seeing his hesitation, his wife increased her groans and moans. The crocodile believed her and reluctantly agreed to his wife's wicked plot.

The next morning, when the husband woke up, he found his wife, sighing and groaning loudly as if she were in great pain. The husband remembered what he had to do that day. With a heavy heart he started from his house assuring his wife that he would bring his friend by noon. The wife smiled wickedly as her husband left.

The crocodile soon reached the rose-apple tree. The monkey was on the tree as usual, jumping from branch to branch and singing, "*Om Sri Ram Jaya Ram Jaya Jaya Ram!*"

As he listened to the devout singing of his innocent friend, the crocodile's heart skipped a beat, but what could he do? The choice was between his wife's life or his friend's. He stood under the tree in the water and looked up. "Hello, my dear friend, good morning to you."

"Good morning to you too, my friend. What's new?" asked the monkey.

"Nothing new, but I have a request. You know, now and then I take the fruit you give me home for my wife. She enjoys it a lot and has been saying that we must invite you for lunch one of these days. Today she implored me to bring you to our place without fail. Will you come?" replied the crocodile.

At the mention of lunch the monkey's mouth watered. Who wouldn't like a good meal? But there was a hitch. "How can I reach your house? I don't know how to swim", said the monkey.

The crocodile replied, "That's no problem. You just jump on to my back. I shall carry you there."

The monkey was very happy. He jumped on to the crocodile's back in a trice, and the crocodile started swimming home. The monkey was in a great mood, thinking of all the dainty eatables which he would get for lunch. He ran up and down the crocodile's back singing gleefully. Seeing the happiness of his innocent friend, the crocodile felt guilty and ashamed. Tears rolled down his cheeks. The monkey saw them with concerned surprise. "Why are you shedding tears, dear friend? Is something amiss?" The crocodile could no longer keep quiet. "Forgive me, my friend, I have deceived you. I am not taking you for

lunch, but to kill you." Then he went on to explain how his wife had a severe headache, for which the doctor had prescribed the paste of a monkey's heart. He concluded, "As soon as we reach my home, my wife is going to kill you to take out your heart and make it into a pulp. I am very sorry to have tricked you into this, but I hope you will understand."

The poor monkey's heart stood still. What an ugly trick to play upon a trusting friend! How

was he to escape? By now, they were in the middle of the river and the monkey could not jump into the water because he did not know how to swim. Who could come to his rescue? The monkey could only remember his beloved Lord Sri Ram. *"Om Sri Ram Jaya Ram Jaya Jaya Ram."*

Closing his eyes, he fervently prayed to the Lord to show him a way out of his predicament. How can those who take shelter at the feet of the Lord be helpless? The Lord is the strength of the weak and the support of the helpless.

So, when the monkey prayed, the Lord gave him solace and strength, and he could think calmly. Suddenly he had a brainwave. He burst out laughing. The crocodile was surprised. How could the monkey laugh in the face of death? He asked, "My dear friend, I thought that you would be either angry with me or terribly frightened at what I have told you. How is it that you are laughing instead? Aren't you afraid of dying?"

The monkey pretended to control his laughter and said, "Oh no, friend. I am not angry with you. After all, when your wife is ill, it is natural for you to get her medicine. How can I find fault with you? But I could not control my laughter because all your efforts are in vain. My heart is not with me now. Had you told me in the beginning, I would have brought it with me. Now, your taking me to your home is futile."

"How so?"enquired the credulous crocodile. "Where is your heart?"

"You see, it's like this. I'm terribly afraid of the water, as you know. When you asked me to jump on to your back, I felt that my heart might get wet in the water. So I removed it and kept it on a branch of the tree for safety. What is the use of your carrying me to your home without my heart?" said the monkey.

"Yes, what is the use?" agreed the foolish crocodile, who had a big body but no brain. "What shall we do now?" he asked the monkey.

The monkey smiled and said, "There is only one way out. Turn back and take me to my tree. I shall climb up and get my heart for you."

The crocodile, happy at this solution, turned back towards the tree. The monkey's heart was thumping with trepidation. At last, when they reached the river bank, the crocodile stopped and said, "Friend, please go up and throw down your heart."

"In a minute," said the monkey jumping up to the safety of the tree. There he scampered up and down the branches in joyous relief, offering his grateful prostrations to the Lord who had saved him from death.

The crocodile waited patiently under the tree for a long time. When it was getting very late and there was no sign of the monkey's heart, he raised his head and asked, "Friend, have you forgotten about giving me your heart? Please throw it down so that I can take it to my wife."

The monkey laughed uproariously and said, "You silly crocodile, what a fool you are to believe that I could have taken out my heart! Go away from here and never show me your face again. False friends like you should never be trusted. Today, God has saved me. I shall never speak to you again!"

THE REAL SACRIFICE

After the great war of the Mahabharata, Dharmaraja, the eldest of the Pandavas, ascended the throne of the Kurus and his four brothers served him faithfully.

Hundreds of thousands of warriors had died in the war. Many women were widowed and children were orphaned. There was a great pall of sorrow and gloom all around and wailing rent the air. In those days, kings used to perform great sacrifices to please the gods and seek peace of mind, on such occasions. Dharmaraja therefore performed a *yajna* to bring peace to the kingdom.

The *yajna* took place for a number of days. Hundreds of Brahmins chanted the sacred mantras and poured oblations into the holy fire. Thousands were fed daily. Wealth, clothes and cattle were freely distributed to one and all. The water used for such charities flowed like a river in spate. All over the kingdom people praised this as the greatest sacrifice ever performed.

One day, when Dharmaraja was thus distributing wealth, a strange mongoose appeared from somewhere. One side of his body was golden and the other side was the usual grey. He rolled in the waters two or three times and muttered to himself in human words, "No, no, this is nothing in comparison to Sakthuprastha's sacrifice. No, nothing at all!"

Everybody present was astounded. A mongoose speaking like a human being and deprecating the great sacrifice of Dharmaraja! Could there be a greater sacrifice than this one, where nothing was lacking?

Dharmaraja bent down and asked the mongoose, "O strange mongoose, you appear to be extraordinary. Who are you? How did you get the ability to speak like a man? Who is the Mahatma Sakthuprastha, of whose sacrifice you speak? We are eager to listen to his story. Please tell us about him.

The mongoose turned to him and replied, "Emperor! I am happy that you want to hear his story. For, such is his glory and piety that even speaking of it again and again, I am not content. Listen and decide for yourself whether I spoke the truth or not.

"Long, long ago, even before the time of your forefathers, there lived in Kurukshetra a poor Brahmin called Sakthuprastha. He had a wife, son and daughter-in-law. They lived by begging. Despite their utter poverty, they were content and never coveted riches. Even in their poverty they were very hospitable and never turned away a guest without offering him food. Any guest was as a god to them and whenever a guest came to eat with them they considered themselves very fortunate.

Then the great famine came. Food was scarce everywhere and Sakthuprastha had great difficulty getting food for his family. Now and then they could get a few grains by gleaning in the fields but often they had to remain without food for days together.

One day, after starving without food for many days, Sakthuprastha got a little flour from somewhere. With a great feeling of relief his wife soon cooked it and all of them sat down to eat, after dividing it into four equal shares. Lo! Before they could commence, a poor Brahmin in torn clothes appeared at their door looking famished and hungry. All of them rejoiced at the sight of the guest. They rose and welcomed him. They brought water and washed his hands and feet. Sakthuprastha then invited him to partake of their food and bless them. The guest was only too eager to oblige them. He readily agreed and took the seat offered to him. But where was the spare food for the guest?

Sakthuprastha brought his share of food and with great reverence placed it before him. The guest who was very hungry, soon finished it. The hosts could see that his hunger was not satisfied and he needed some more food. Sakthuprastha's wife called him aside and pointing to her share of the food, requested her husband to offer it to the guest.

Sakthuprastha felt very sad. He said, "My virtuous wife, it is the duty of a husband to feed his wife and children and sustain them. For a number of days there has been no food in the house and you have been starving. How can I deprive you of your food now?" "Lord, am I separate from you? Is it not equally my duty to participate and share in your duties, joys and sorrows? When a guest comes to our house it is our duty to satisfy him. Please don't hesitate but offer this food to him," she replied.

Considering himself fortunate to have a wife who encouraged him in doing his duty, Sakthuprastha placed his wife's share of the food before the guest, who ate it very quickly. But alas, he was still casting hungry looks all around.

Sakthuprastha's son then came up to his father and said in a low tone, "Father, the scriptures say that the son is the reflection of his father. I am duty bound to discharge all your debts. The duty towards a guest is the greatest debt which we should discharge. O Father, please offer my food to the venerable guest, so that my duty can be fulfilled."

Sakthuprastha was reluctant to deprive his young son of his food. But he had to give in to his request. So he placed his son's food also before the guest and requested him to eat it. Unmindful of what was happening, the guest ate it all and again looked up for more.

Then Sakthuprastha's daughter-in-law came forward with her share of the food and said, "Arya, I am the better half of my husband and all his obligations are mine too. Please offer my food to the guest and satisfy his hunger."

Sakthuprastha was in great misery. In a choking voice he said, "My daughter, I brought you from your father's house, promising to look after you like my own daughter. But here you are, always starving and famished. Your delicate frame has grown emaciated. Let me not commit a further sin by taking away your food."

The daughter-in-law replied, "Don't grieve, dear Father, I am the daughter of the house and have to share all its joys and sorrows. Only by doing my duty can I attain *punya*. Please be merciful to me and accept this food."

Sakthuprastha took the food from her hands and placed it before the guest. As the guest was

eating, they were all apprehensive lest he should still be hungry after eating this too, for there was not a morsel more in the house to offer. But their fears were groundless. There was a look of replete satisfaction on the face of the Brahmin as he ate the food, and when it was finished he got up to wash his hands.

Rejoicing that the guest could be fed to his satisfaction, Sakhthuprastha came forward and

washed his hands and feet. Lo! As he did so, the poor Brahmin in tatters vanished and in his place stood a radiant god, looking kindly at the whole family and smiling benignly. His smile lit up the entire house.

Greatly wondering at this transformation, the family stood in awestruck wonder, not knowing what to make of it. Then the god himself spoke, "Don't be surprised, O Sakthuprastha. I am Lord Yama and I came to test you. I am pleased with you all. You need no longer stay in this miserable world of sorrows and troubles. You will immediately be taken to *Vaikuntha* to stay permanently in the blissful presence of Lord Narayana."

Thus relating the story of Sakthuprastha's rare sacrifice, the mongoose added, "O Dharmaraja, crouched in a hole in that house, I saw and heard everything that took place there. When everybody left, I crawled out of the hole to eat the crumbs that were lying on the ground. As I ate, my body touched the water on the ground, with which Sakthuprastha had washed the feet of the guest. Instantaneously that part of my body which had touched the water turned to gold, as you can see. The crumbs that I ate gave me the power to speak like a human being. See how holy the sacrifice of the Brahmin and his family was. It was a true *yajna*! It was true sacrifice, and true austerity!

Ever since I have been wandering all over the earth and dipping myself in the holy waters wherever a sacrifice is performed, hoping to turn the rest of my body into gold too. But to no avail. As you saw today, I dipped myself in the holy waters here too. But my colour remains the same.

That is why I said that this was nothing compared to the sacrifice of Sakthuprastha," the mongoose said in conclusion. Dharmaraja was filled with great joy and exclaimed, "O mongoose, today is a great day for me since I could listen to the story of a man as pious as Sakthuprastha. Verily no sacrifice could be greater than his. His is the true sacrifice! His is the true austerity."

KING SIBI'S COMPASSION

Once upon a time there lived a great king called Sibi. He was very kind and charitable and became very famous for his generosity. His fame spread all over the earth and even reached the heavens.

The Lord of Heaven, Indra wanted to test him and see if King Sibi was really as great as his fame made him out him to be.

So Indra and Agni started out from Heaven. Agni assumed the form of a dove and Indra, of a fierce hawk. Agni flew ahead, his wings fluttering as though terrified and Indra followed at a distance, as if in hot pursuit. They flew straight to the palace of King Sibi.

Sibi was in the garden distributing alms to the poor. The little fluttering, frightened dove came and perched upon his wrist, looking at him with tearful eyes full of fear. Sibi immediately took her in his hands. Stroking her back kindly, he said, "Don't be afraid, little dove, I won't let any harm befall you."

Just as he was saying this, the hawk swooped down, angry and haughty, and tried to snatch the dove from the king's hands. But the king

raised his hand in a flash and stopped the hawk. The hawk glared at the king angrily and spoke in a human voice, "This dove is my prey. I have been pursuing it since morning. Why do you deny me my food, O King?"

Surprised at hearing the hawk speak like a man, Sibi replied, "I do not know who you are, O Hawk, who can speak like a man. This poor frightened dove has sought my protection. It is my duty to save her from all harm. I won't allow you to snatch her away from me and make her your prey."

The hawk then argued, "Rajan, you are renowned as a kind king. Perhaps it is your duty to protect those in distress. But is your kindness limited only to the dove? What about me? Am I not equally entitled to claim your pity? I am a bird of prey, who can live only by eating the meat of smaller creatures. By depriving me of my food, are you not condemning me to die? Is this your dharma?"

King Sibi was in a dilemma. This hawk could not only speak like a human being, but also argue like one! Evidently his duty was towards both the dove and the hawk. He thought for a while. At last he said, "Hawk, what you say is true. I won't deprive you of your food. But at the same time I can't give up this poor, frightened dove. Will you accept some other flesh as a substitute?"

The hawk replied, "Very well, King, I have no objection as long as my hunger is satisfied. But you must give me flesh exactly equal to that of the dove. I won't accept less." Then mockingly he added, "But where will you get the substitute flesh from? Will you take another life to save the life of this dove?"

Stung, Sibi retorted instantly, "No, no, I won't think of harming another life. I will give you my own flesh in place of the dove." He then turned to his attendants and ordered them to bring a balance. The attendants accordingly brought the balance and erected it before the King. Sibi placed the dove on one side of the balance. He took out his sword and cutting small portions of his flesh, placed them on the other side. But how strange! The dove, which looked so small and frail in the weighing scales, was always heavier! King Sibi went on cutting portion after portion from his body and placing it in the balance... yet to no purpose... till at last no more flesh remained for him to cut. Wondering at the weight of the dove, Sibi then threw away his sword and himself mounted the balance. Lo! Now the balance was quite equal. Rejoicing that he was at last able to give the hawk its due, Sibi turned to the hawk and said, "O Hawk, my weight is equal to the weight of the dove. Please eat me and spare the dove."

As he said these words, there was appreciative applause from the gods who had gathered in the sky to witness the test. They beat the heavenly drums and showered flowers on the king. The hawk and the dove shed their assumed forms and stood before him in their shining glorious forms. Sibi gazed at them in amazement.

Indra said, "O great and generous king, know that we are Indra and Agni, come down from Heaven to test you. You have indeed proved yourself to be greater than your fame. You will be blessed with a long life and vast riches. Your name will be remembered in the world as long as the sun and the moon remain."

So saying, Indra touched Sibi with his hand. Lo! All the cuts and wounds vanished from Sibi's body and he stood there whole again, as strong as ever. He bowed to the gods with great devotion, and they blessed him and returned to their abodes.

ADI KAVI VALMIKI

Thousands of years ago, there was a hunter who lived by robbing and looting people. He lived in a jungle with his wife and children and no traveller who passed through the jungle was safe. If the need arose, he didn't hesitate to kill innocent pilgrims and rob them.

One day, Devarshi Narada was passing through the forest. As usual, the robber was on the look-out for victims and as soon as he saw the sage approaching, joyously singing and playing on his veena, he thought he would be an easy victim. He jumped down from the branch of a tree where he had been hiding and landed with a thud just in front of the sage. Flashing his sword, he threatened, "Give me all that you possess. Otherwise I will kill you."

Narada was the son of Brahma Deva himself and he was never afraid of anyone. He saw God in all and loved all. Looking kindly into the eyes of the hunter he asked, "Why do you want to kill me? I have never harmed you."

The robber replied, "It is not because of anything you did that I want to rob you. I want your wealth to maintain my wife and children. If you try to stop me I will kill you."

Narada was unperturbed by his threatening attitude. He said, "Very well, my boy, you may do as you please. But please tell me one thing. You say that you are committing this sin for the sake of your wife and children. They are sharing the wealth earned by you, but will they share the sins that you are earning too?"

The robber was confused. He had never thought of the matter in this light before. He replied, "Of course, they will have to. Why else should I commit sins for their sake?"

Narada shook his head in disagreement and said, "No, they will not. If you have any doubts, go and ask your wife and children." The robber was suspicious that Narada might be playing a trick on him to escape. He said sternly, "No, I won't leave you and go. You are just trying to hoodwink me and escape."

Laughing at his suspicions Narada assured him, "No, my son, I promise you that I won't escape. I will surely wait for you till you return. If you don't believe me, tie me to one of these trees and go to your house."

The robber bound Narada tightly to a nearby tree and hurried home. Ever since the sage had

asked him the strange question, his mind had been disturbed. Had he been ruining himself with sins to no purpose?

He went home and calling his wife and children, said "My dears, you know I have been earning wealth by robbing and killing, to maintain you all. You have been sharing all that I earned. Won't you share the sins earned by me also?" The wife and children were horrified at this suggestion. They said, "We are your dependents and it is your duty to maintain us. We never asked you to commit sins to earn wealth. If you choose to commit sins, it is your own lookout. How are we concerned with it? You alone will have to bear the consequences of your sins."

The eyes of the robber were suddenly opened. He realised that he had been accumulating terrible sins, from which there was no escape. Why should he lead a sinful life for these people? He ran back to Narada and hastily untying his bonds, fell at his feet. Beside himself with grief, he begged, "Mahatma, in my ignorance I have committed many sins. Please tell me how I can redeem myself. I no more desire to lead this life of sin. Pray, save me."

Narada rejoiced at his transformation. He lifted the robber to his feet and told him, "Fear not, my son. There is one name, the *Taraka*, which redeems even the greatest of sinners. Repeat the name with all your heart and soul. All your sins will soon be washed away." He then whispered in his ear the sacred name, "Rama" and asked the robber to repeat it.

His whole life had been spent in doing and saying only harsh things. So the robber could not utter the word "Rama" try as he might. But Narada was too kind to leave him. So he tried another method. He slowly uttered the word "Ma ra", inverting the sacred name. This time the robber could pronounce the letters, "Ma ra, Ma ra..." And he started repeating the letters in quick succession... "Ma ra, Ma ra, Ma... Ra. ..Ma Ra... Ma... Ra.. ma... Ra ma... Rama... Rama..." Thus, after a time without his realising it, the robber was repeating the *Taraka nama*. He was captivated by the charm of the sacred name and he went on repeating the name, forgetting his surroundings. He sat like that continuously without moving and without opening his eyes and years passed. Seeing him sitting like an immovable stone, ants, worms and insects crawled fearlessly near him and on him and built their homes and nests. The anthills grew and grew until they covered him fully and he could not even be seen.

This undisturbed *tapas* washed off all his sins and at last he gained a vision of the Lord. Overflowing with great joy and bliss, he rose from his seat, shedding the anthills around him.

As he rose from the anthills— 'Valmika' as they are called in Sanskrit— he came to be called Valmiki.

Since then Maharshi Valmiki lived on the banks of the Ganges in an ashram of his own. He led a simple, pious life, bathing in the sacred river and eating dried roots and the fruits of the forest. He was in tune with the peace and beauty of the forest and was always in an elevated state.

One day while he was returning from the river after his morning bath, he saw a pair of Krouncha birds, flying joyously in the sky in love play. He was charmed by the innocent joy of the birds and continued to look at them in blissful rapture. Just then an arrow struck the male bird in the heart and it fell down bleeding, with a piteous cry. Seeing her mate gone, the female bird arose in great grief and flew round and round his body, moaning and shrieking. The bird's wordless grief was so pitiable, that the kindly sage's heart was touched. Tears came to his eyes and he felt all the misery of the small bird in his own heart. He looked around and saw a hunter crouching nearby. In infinite mercy and sorrow, Valmiki cried out—

"A future, O hunter, none will you have
For killing the Krouncha in the midst of love."

Then he suddenly stopped, surprised at his own words. For this was not his usual way of speaking... these words contained a rhythm and a melody. He realised that it was a poem that had come out of his heart's anguish, the first poem that he had ever composed. In fact, it was the first sloka in the history of the world, for no one had written any poetry till then.

Later he wrote the *Ramayana*, the story of the incarnation of Lord Vishnu as Rama in melodious, beautiful verse. It is sung reverently by all Hindus, even though thousands of years have passed since it was composed. Valmiki is acclaimed as the Adi Kavi, the first poet and is gratefully remembered by all poets when they begin to compose a new poem.

KARNA'S CHARITY

Once upon a time there lived a king called Dhritarashtra, who ruled over Hastinapura. He had a vast empire and a hundred sons. His eldest son's name was Duryodhana.

Duryodhana had a friend called Karna, who was the king of a small kingdom called Anga Desa.

Karna was very kind-hearted and charitable. Anybody's request for help was sure to get fulfilled, for Karna never said 'no' to anyone. He started his day with distribution of money, cattle, land and other things to people. Every day a long queue of needy people could be seen in front of his palace even before dawn. Getting all that they needed, they would return from the palace loudly praising Karna's charitable nature. Duryodhana's palace was nearby. So the lavish praise bestowed on Karna reached his ears every day. He began to grow increasingly jealous. He thought, "After all, Karna is a petty king with small riches at his disposal. I am far richer than he is and I can give much more than he can give. So I should become more famous than him."

Resolving thus, he started to give a lot of charity to the poor. Soon he became famous and people began to praise him too. But he was not satisfied because Karna was still held in greater esteem than he was.

Indra, the king of the Devas, knew what was passing through Duryodhana's mind and decided to teach him a lesson. He came down to earth disguised as a poor Brahmin and went to Duryodhana's court. Pompously Duryodhana asked, "O Brahmin, what help do you want of me? Ask for anything, please. I am at your service to give you whatever you want. Do not hesitate even if it is a big thing, for I can afford to give you anything that you may need."

Laughing inwardly at the pompous words, the Brahmin replied, "Prince, I do not need much. I am going to perform a *yajna* shortly, for which I require a lot of fuel. Please give me enough fuel for this purpose. That will be enough for me."

Duryodhana laughed aloud and said, "O poor Brahmin, what can I say of your luck? You come to a great prince and ask only for fuel. Let it be so. This is all your good luck. Take as much fuel as you please."

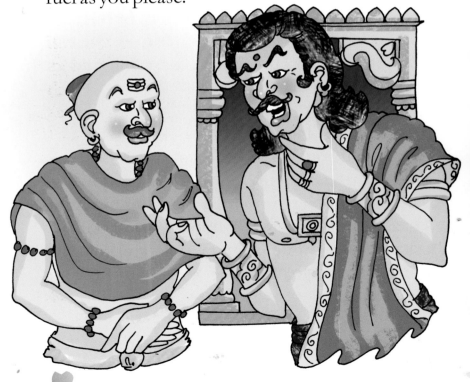

The Brahmin appeared very pleased and praised Duryodhana gratefully. He said, "O charitable prince! My *yajna* will start in ten days. I will come and take the fuel on that day, for I do not have a place to store the fuel." Duryodhana agreed and the Brahmin left.

Now, Indra was not only the king of the Devas, he had supremacy over the clouds and rains also. He could, at will, order the rains to pour down. He ordered that there should be an incessant, heavy downpour of rain for the next ten days. The rains came down heavily, in torrents, without a single minute's respite for all of ten days. The tanks and wells were filled, rivers flowed in spate, and all over the earth there was a wide sheet of water. Everything was drenched and not a single thing remained dry.

Ten days passed. The rains came to a stop suddenly and the smiling sun rose as usual, brightening the gloomy atmosphere of the past ten days. Indra disguised himself again as the poor Brahmin and came to Duryodhana early in the morning. He said, "Prince, my *yajna* will start today. Please give me the promised fuel."

Duryodhana stared at the Brahmin in dismay. Not that he did not want to give the fuel, but he was helpless at that particular time because there was no dry fuel available anywhere. With an apologetic look he said, "Please excuse me Brahmin. Because of these terrible rains, all the fuel is drenched. Not a piece of dry wood is available now. Please postpone your *yajna* for some days. As soon as the fuel is dry, I will give you as much as you need."

The Brahmin looked very disappointed. With a rueful face, he exclaimed, "O Duryodhana, is this how great people keep their word? Did you not promise to give me the fuel this day? How can I postpone the *yajna* to another day? It can be performed only on auspicious days. Today is best suited for the *yajna*. You must fulfill your promise. "

Duryodhana was annoyed. He was feeling guilty within, but he did not want to concede that he was in the wrong. The Brahmin's insistence made matters worse. Losing his temper he said, "Are you mad? How do you expect me to fulfil a promise under these conditions? Go away from here if you can't listen to reason."

The Brahmin made a wry face and cried out, "Mad indeed! A pious Brahmin wishing to perform a *yajna*, appears to you as mad! Of course I must have been mad to have come to you with my request instead of going to Karna. He would never have broken a promise, like you. Anyway no harm is done. Even now I can go to him and ask for the fuel. I am sure to get it from him." So saying, the Brahmin immediately left Duryodhana's palace and went to Karna. Duryodhana was very chagrined to think that the Brahmin thought better of Karna than of him, but he consoled himself, thinking that even Karna wouldn't be able to procure dry fuel. He would have to say 'no' to the Brahmin. Then the Brahmin of course would be similarly angry with Karna and curse him too!

As he was thus thinking hopefully, the Brahmin went and stood before Karna. Karna made obeisance to him and asked, "O best of Brahmins, how can I serve you?" The Brahmin blessed him and said, "O Karna, I need fuel for performing a *yajna* today. Please give me sufficient fuel."

Karna grew thoughtful. Surely there must be some way to get what the Brahmin needed! A *yajna* was an auspicious sacrifice, which couldn't be postponed. Thinking hard, he raised his head and his glance fell on the rafters and beams supporting the roof. These at least were dry enough. In a flash it occurred to him how to provide the dry fuel. He called his servants and ordered them to break down one of the buildings in the palace compound and, carefully gather the beams, rafters and the wooden portion of the roof. He got all of it loaded on to the carts. Soon there was enough wood for the *yajna*. Then the load was carefully covered with animal skins so that it wouldn't get wet on the

way. Happy that he was able to provide what the Brahmin needed, he came up to the Brahmin and said, "Good Sir, your fuel is ready. Please instruct the men where to take it." Filled with great joy and admiration, the Brahmin blessed him and left, loudly singing Karna's praises.

As he passed Duryodhana's palace, Duryodhana eagerly came out to see how Karna had fared. When he heard the Brahmin's

praises he was filled with surprise and could not believe his ears. He was very eager to know where Karna had got the dry fuel. So, swallowing his pride, he asked the Brahmin how Karna had procured the fuel. The Brahmin told him how Karna had got one of his buildings pulled down and given him sufficient fuel for the *yajna*. He then raised a corner of the skins on the carts and showed him the rafters and beams.

Duryodhana realised how truly charitable Karna was, and how mean he was in being jealous of Karna. He learnt that true charity lay not in riches, but in a heart that has love, compassion and sympathy for all fellow beings. From that moment, he gave up being jealous of Karna and started loving him like a true friend.